To everyone (who has or is)
raising kids without their pillars,
this is for you.

MASCOT KIDS!
an imprint of Amplify Publishing Group
www.mascotbooks.com

# A Letter to My Kids



For more information, please contact:
Mascot Kids, an imprint of Amplify Publishing Group
620 Herndon Parkway #220
Herndon, VA 20170
info@mascotbooks.com

CPSIA Code: PRKF0323A
Library of Congress Control Number: 2022915988
ISBN-13: 978-1-63755-149-3

Printed in China

# A Letter to My Kids

Amanda Sporrer

Illustrated by Maria Ballarin

# To my children,

It's been some time since my daddy (Pap, to you guys) went to heaven, and I wanted to write down some of my feelings about my dad so you can read them in years to come.

If you come to love me half as much as I love my parents, then I would be truly blessed. Now that my daddy is gone (although he will never be gone from my heart), I know how true that is.

My dad was my friend and my idol. Everything I have done in my life, I did with the hope that he would be proud of me.

I know he was proud of me, and for that I will always be grateful.

I will always miss him, but I know that whatever I do for the rest of my life, I will always think about how he would feel about it.

The times I spent with my parents were some of my happiest. I looked forward, more than anything, to being with them and my family. I hope you feel, or come to feel, the same way.

Sometimes Pap was tough to get along with, but only on the little things, like helping him work on a project. He had his ways, just like I do, and on the little things, Pap wanted his way.

On the big stuff, the stuff that really mattered, Pap was a rock . . . a completely unselfish rock. He would do whatever it took to help his children.

I think about all the things my parents had to give up, or do without, so they could give to me and my sibling. I will try to do the same, but I know it will be very hard for me to be as unselfish.

If you can come to feel about me like I felt about my daddy, then I will rate my life a success. Daddy was always there for me, and I always wanted him there for me.

Me and Kids, 2020

I will
try to always
be there for you. I
know I won't do as good
a job as Pap did for me . . .
**but I will try.**

Remember Pap, because there will never be another like him.

Love,
mommy

# About the Author

**AMANDA SPORRER** is a former special education teacher turned stay-at-home mom. At the age of twenty-six, she tragically lost her dad. To help with her daily grief, Amanda turned to writing, and *A Letter to My Kids* was born. Amanda lives in Pittsburgh, Pennsylvania, with her husband, three children, and dog.